THE CREATIVE COLOURING BOOK FOR GROWN-UPS

Michael O'Mara Books Limited

First published in Great Britain in 2012 by
Michael O'Mara Books Limited
9 Lion Yard
Tremadoc Road
London SW4 7NQ

A CIP catalogue record for this book is available from the British Library.

Papers used by Michael O'Mara Books Limited are natural, recyclable products made from wood grown in sustainable forests. The manufacturing processes conform to the environmental regulations of the country of origin.

ISBN: 978-1-84317-869-9

14

www.mombooks.com

www.shutterstock.com

Designed by Ana Bjezancevic

Printed and bound in Spain

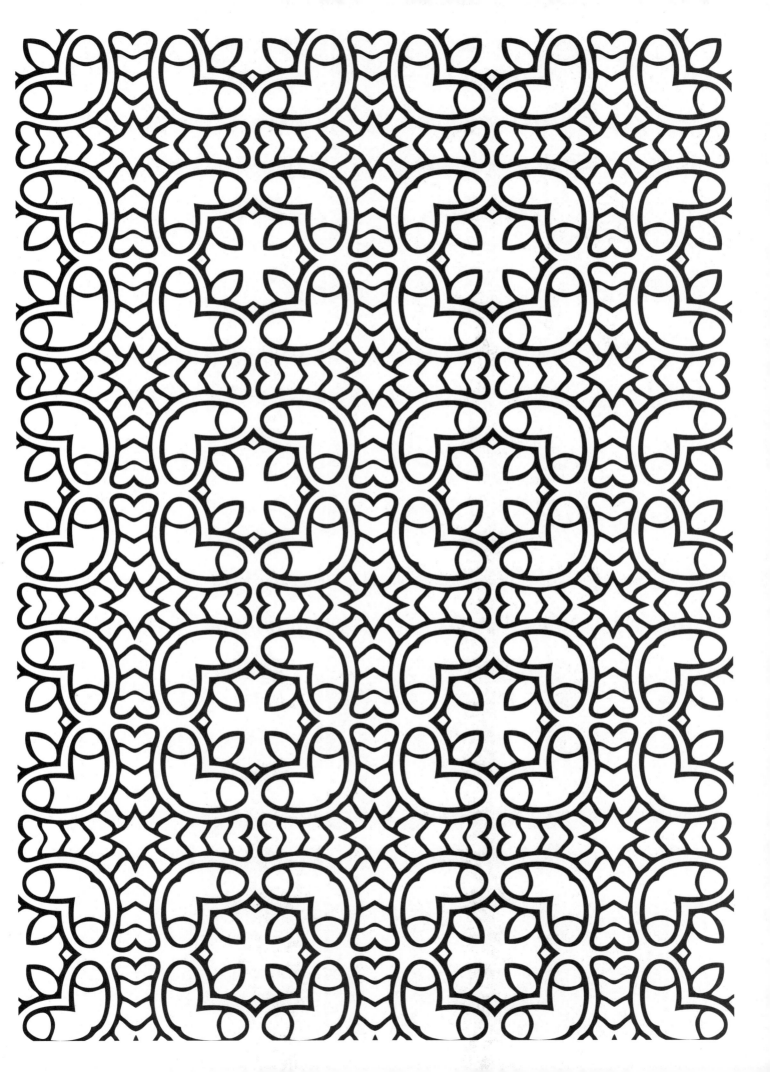

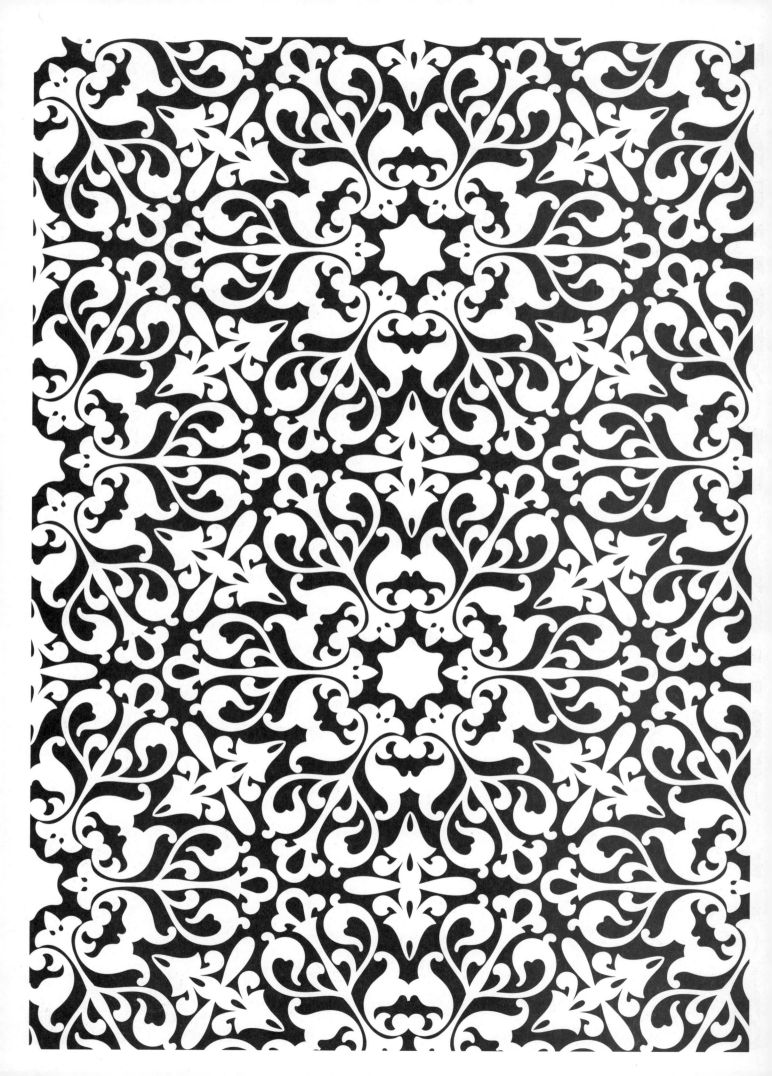

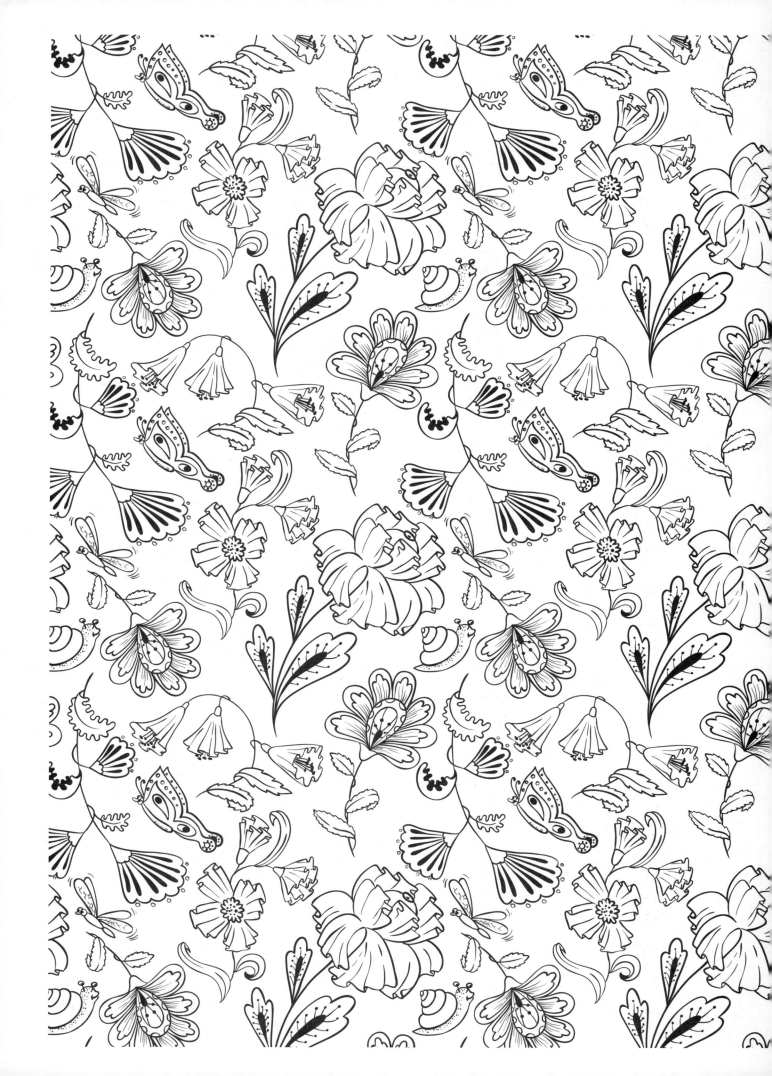

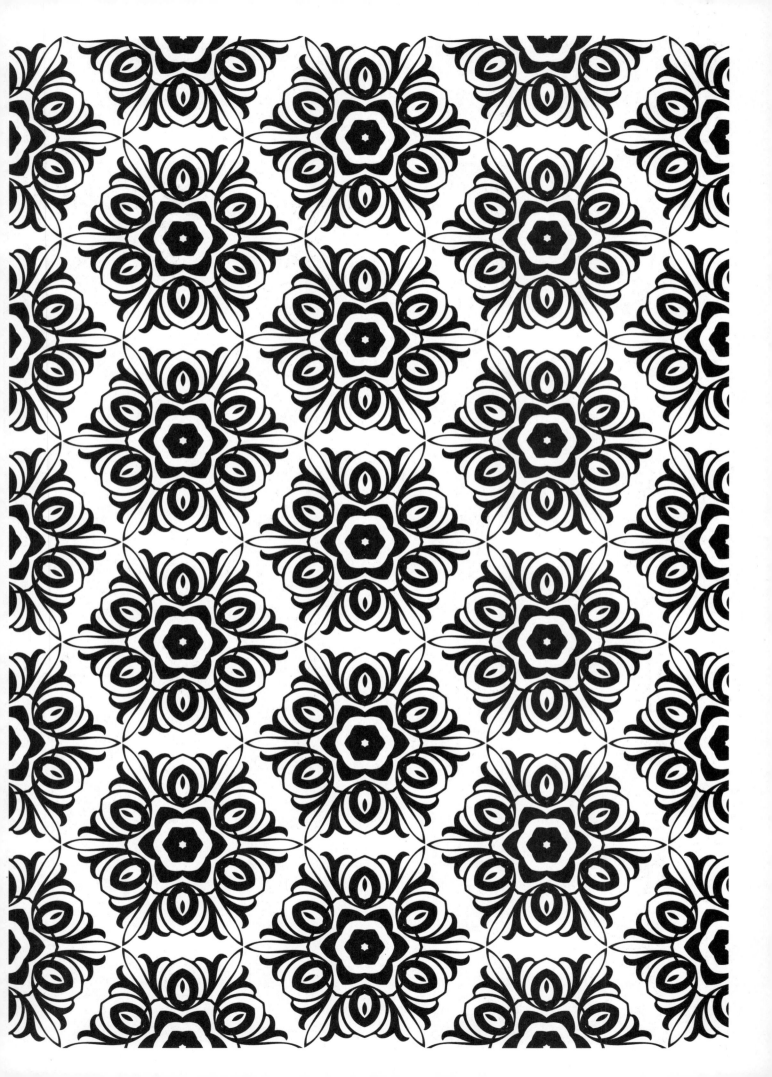

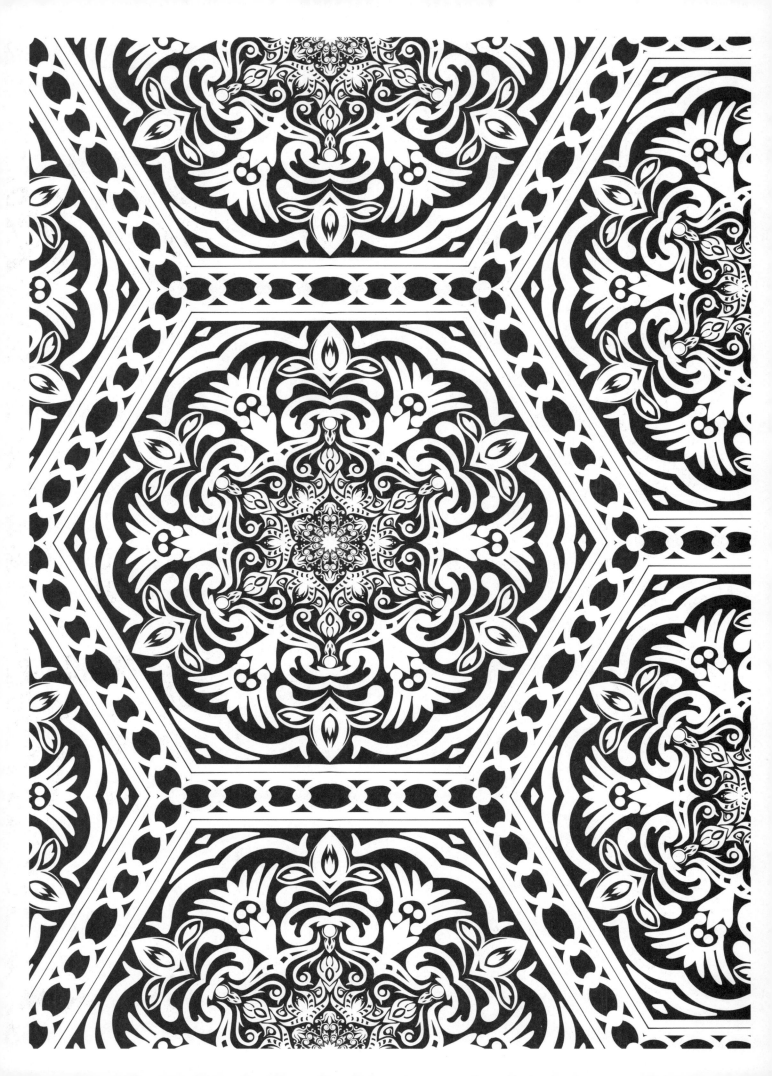

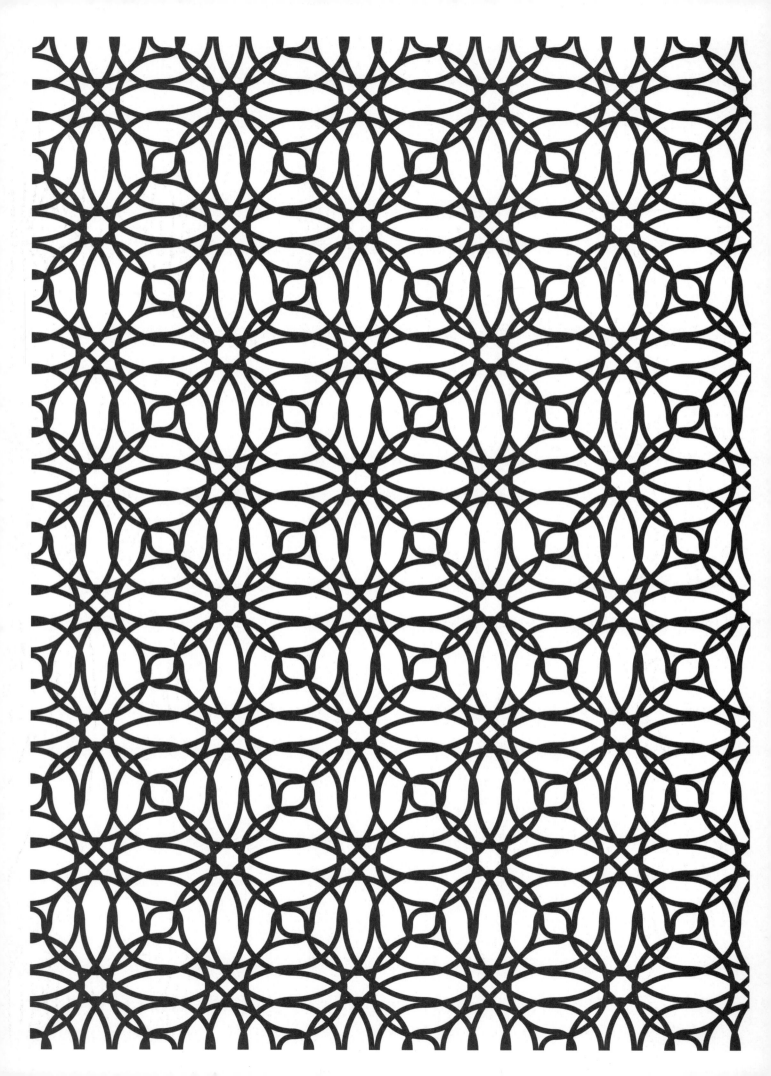

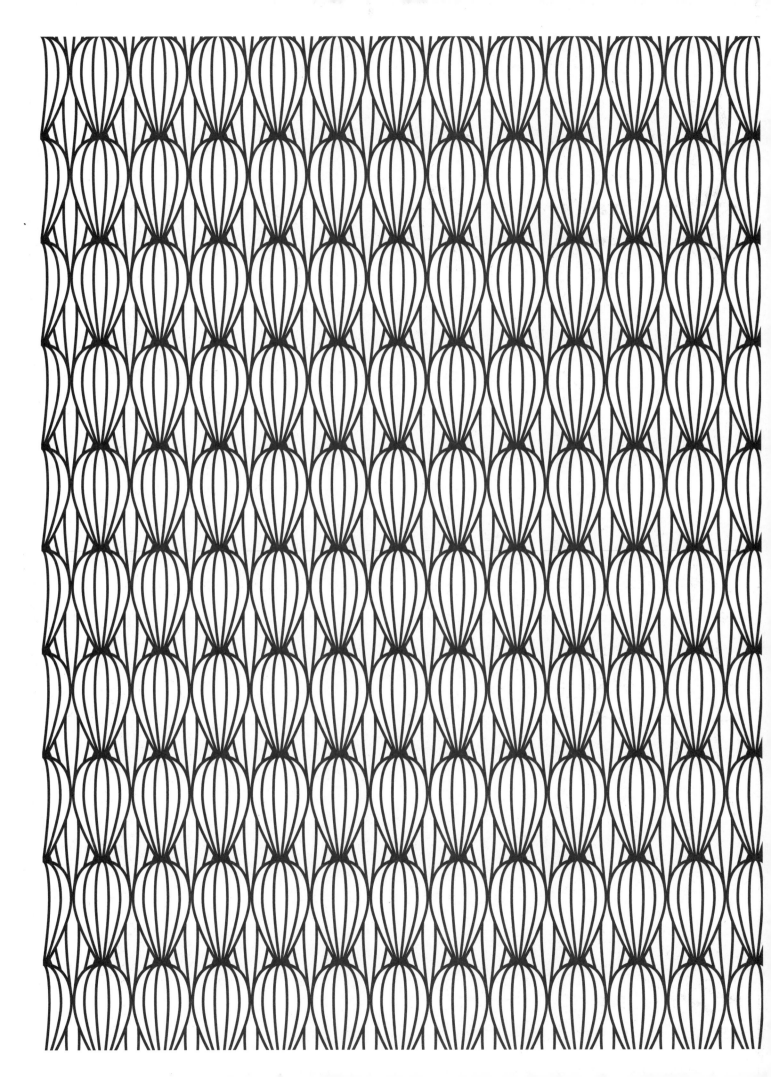

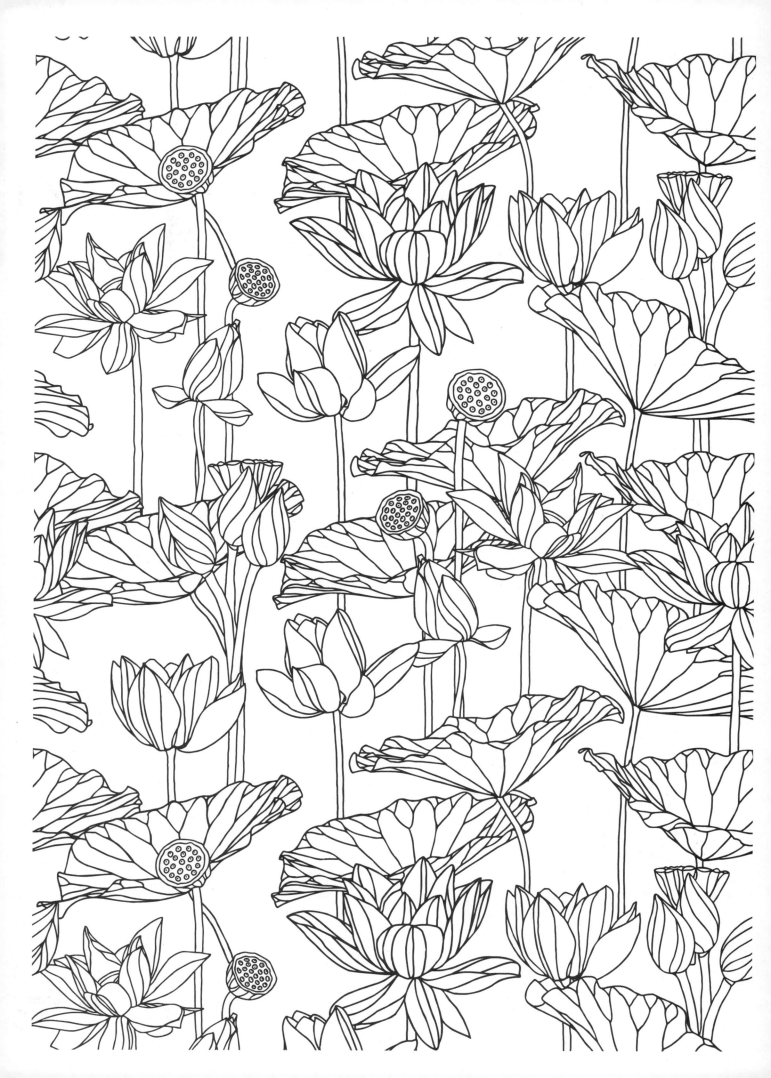

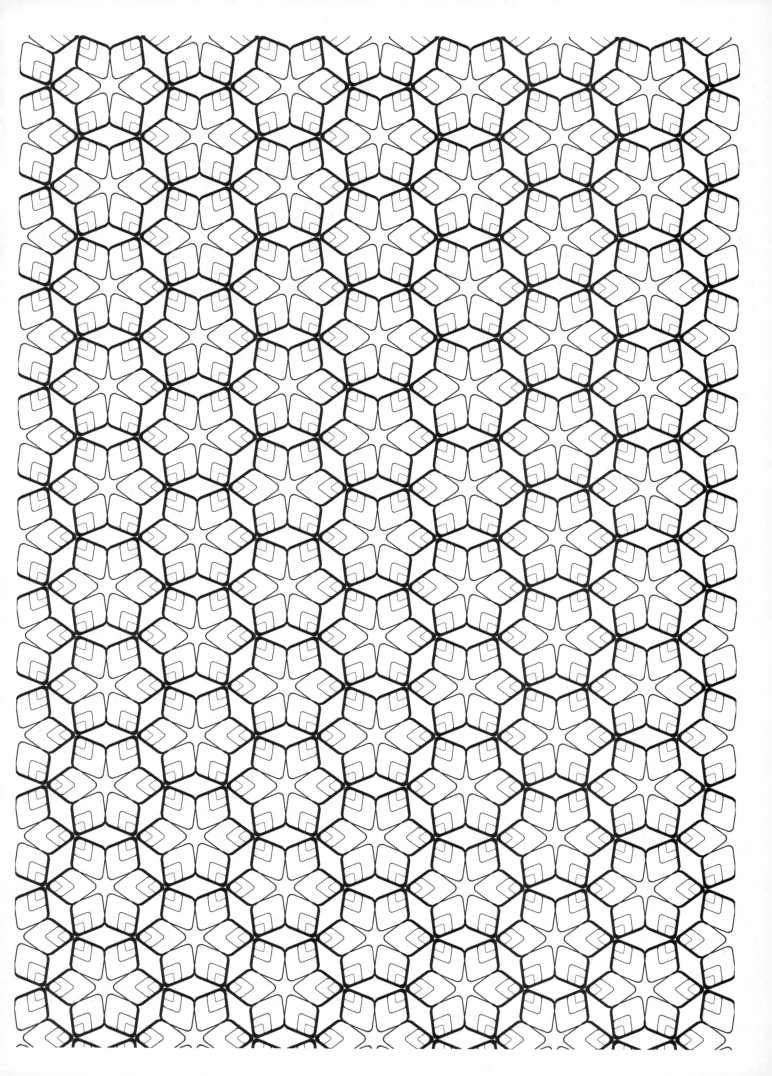

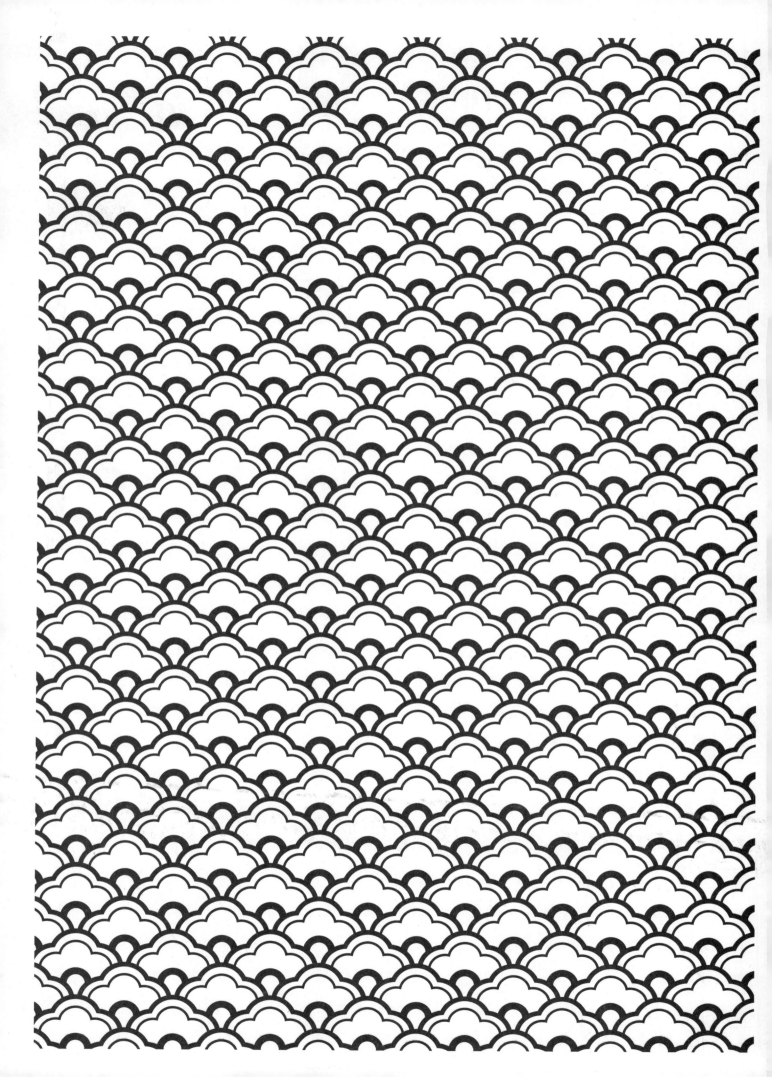